The Weight of Grace
Reflections from the Center

Book II of *The Weight Trilogy*

By

Chetan Rao

On the M.A.R.C. Publishers
(www.onthemarcpub.com)

Copyright Page

First Edition, 2026

The Weight of Grace – Reflections from the Center
ISBN: 979-8-9936911-3-8
Cover design by the author
Printed in the United States of America

Dedication

Dedicated to our parents, and ancestors, without whom, we would be nothing.

Epigraph

To walk toward another is to walk toward yourself; every step becomes a form of truth.

Foreword

This book listens where others might speak.

You do not need to understand everything here, to be changed by it.

It is a story of grace in ordinary moments,

and the slow work of becoming whole.

Renee Angela Smith

Renee Angela Smith is an author and the creator of Kota Bear Books, a children's series rooted in connection and curiosity. She lives in California with her family and writes from the midst of ordinary life.

Prologue
The Story Isn't of Perfection
Not all beginnings announce themselves; some simply open like dawn.

The story doesn't begin with falling in love.

It begins with learning how to stay.

Long before grief carved its quiet chambers into their lives, before daughters filled the house with music and questions, before Karan walked the edge of himself and Diana held the center alone—there was only a girl from a Wisconsin farm who understood silence better than words, and a boy from a faraway country who carried too much of the world inside him.

Their lives didn't meet so much as drift toward each other, like two long currents finally converging.

But grace rarely announces itself.

It doesn't arrive with thunder or prophecy.

It comes softly—

in the steady rhythm of chores before dawn,

in the way dust glows in a kitchen window,

in balconies lit by the warm hush of Mumbai evenings,

in lullabies whispered through hospital corridors,

in the fragile moments when love is not an answer, but a question asked again and again.

This is Diana's story, though she never claimed it.

A story of the middle — of the center — the quiet place from which everything else moves.

Not the fire of the first book, nor the surrender of the last, but the still point between them.

The part of the soul where grace lives when the world tilts.

The part that listens when another cannot speak.

If *The Weight of Shadows* is about surviving the edge,

and *The Weight of Nothing* will be about transcending the heights,

then this is the tale of the space between —

where breath steadies,

where presence gathers,

where love learns to stand without demanding resolution.

In the end, the story isn't of perfection.

It is of presence.

The kind that stays.

The kind that returns.

The kind that endures long after the storms have passed,

quietly illuminating everything it touches.

This is the weight of grace.

Chapter 1
The Farm and the Center
Stillness teaches before the world begins.

Before the sun touched the ridgeline, the farm was already awake.

The air smelled of frost and feed, the kind of cold that cracked the skin at the base of the thumb. Diana pulled her coat close and stepped into the half-light. Steam rose from the cattle like prayer. The barn's wooden ribs glowed faintly under a single yellow bulb, and from inside came the slow percussion of milkers, rubber hoses breathing in rhythm with the cows.

Her father moved through the aisle without a sound. Years of repetition had turned every action into instinct—open gate, clip suction cup, test the seal, rinse the bucket. He nodded when he saw her, the kind of nod that meant both good morning and you know what to do.

Diana did. She had been doing chores since she could walk. By twelve she could repair the separator. By sixteen she could sense a coming freeze from the smell of the wind. The farm clung to her; it was proof of belonging.

Outside, the eastern sky bruised from black to cobalt. Across the field, a single birch shimmered white, its bark catching what little light there was. Her mother's kitchen window glowed faintly in the house beyond the silo. The outline of her moved behind the curtain—coffee, toast, radio news from La Crosse or Madison. Everything in that life was measured by repetition, and repetition, Diana believed, was its own kind of love.

She thought often about that: the difference between habit and faith. Her father prayed every night, but never in church language. His devotion was motion—the sweep of his hand across a cow's flank, the careful folding of invoices, the way he never left a latch unhooked. "Consistency," he said once, "is God's quiet handshake."

She had grown up believing him.

2

When chores ended, she followed him outside to the milk truck. He stood contemplating, face half hidden in the collar of his coat, eyes on the distant road.

"Storm coming," he murmured.

"Tomorrow?" she asked.

He shrugged. "Maybe. Maybe not. You'll know before I do—you're the one with the nose for weather."

Compliments from him came disguised as tasks.

In the kitchen, her mother had already laid out breakfast: eggs glossy with butter, thick toast, a jar of plum preserves labeled in neat blue ink '79. The radio crackled a forecast—cold front moving in from Minnesota, lows in the teens. Diana poured milk into glasses and watched the thin line of cream rise to the top. Her father sat, bowing his head without words. Her mother's hands folded in her lap, still for the first time all morning.

Sometimes Diana wondered what her mother thought about while everyone else was speaking. There was a gentleness to her silence, but also something unsaid, like a room no one entered anymore.

After breakfast, Diana walked to the edge of the property, where the pasture dipped into a small trout stream. The water ran narrow and fast this time of year, and she liked how it carried the reflection of the sky even when the sky itself seemed empty. She crouched and traced a stick through the current. The world looked different upside down, clouds drifting beneath her fingers.

She didn't yet know why she kept coming here—only that the moving water steadied her more than any still pond ever could. Later she would call that instinct grace, though she had no word for it then.

Back at the house, her mother was folding laundry in the living room, the television playing softly. A reporter mentioned something about hostages in Tehran. The world, it seemed, was always either freezing or burning. Diana imagined maps she had seen in geography class—lines of latitude, countries like puzzles—and tried to picture all that distance.

College brochures lay in a stack on the table. She thumbed through one for the University of Wisconsin–Madison: red-brick buildings, a lake shimmering under autumn light, students laughing on a hill. It looked impossibly wide, as though air itself were thinner there.

Her father found her studying the pictures.

"Are you thinking of applying?"

"I already did," she said quietly.

He nodded, not surprised. "Then you'll go."

No discussion, no protest—just that. His acceptance landed heavier than resistance might have.

That night, beneath the weight of quilts, she listened to the house shift and settle. The walls creaked the way old bones do when they remember motion. She felt both anchored and restless, as if her body already knew it would leave.

At dawn she rose again to the rhythm of the barn. Frost glazed the windows, turning each pane into a small white lake. Her breath fogged the air as she led the cows in, the bells on their collars clanging softly like an old hymn. Somewhere in that steady noise she thought she heard her own pulse—slow, patient, waiting.

For now, the center held.

In her graduating class there were twenty-seven students—twenty-eight until Mark Krueger's family moved to Minnesota. In small towns, anonymity wasn't possible; everyone carried everyone else's stories like shared air.

The high school sat on a low hill above the river, its flagpole bent slightly from a storm the year she turned fifteen. The gym smelled of varnish and sweat, the band room of brass and chalk dust. Diana played clarinet in the concert band, a straight-backed player with precise rhythm. Her director called her "the metronome." It embarrassed her, but she liked that it meant she was dependable.

Every summer, she attended band camp north of Eau Claire—dew, scales, bonfire songs. Her first kiss had been there: seventh grade, behind the mess hall, a boy named Brian with braces that flashed in the firelight. Clumsy, almost comic, but afterward she felt something new—an awareness, not excitement. The world, she realized, contained tremors beyond duty.

There were boyfriends later—Tom with his letter jacket, Eric who taught her to drive stick—but none rooted deep. They existed as faces in yearbooks, not memories. She liked to understand before she surrendered.

Her real attachments were to her siblings. David, the oldest, finishing engineering at Madison; Dorothy in nursing there; Doreen two years younger, full of laughter; Drew, six years younger, always muddy and curious. Their voices came home through static on Sunday calls, bright and thin.

Madison, through their letters, shimmered like another planet orbiting the same sun.

Winter came early. The bus heater failed, the roads vanished under snowbanks. In biology she studied dividing cells, comforted by their precision. Yet restlessness stirred—subtle, like wind in the rafters.

After band practice one afternoon, she lingered in the hallway, reading the map of graduates' destinations. Most pins clustered close—Milwaukee, Eau Claire, La Crosse. A few stretched farther. She touched the one marked Madison. Dorothy's pin. David's pin. Maybe hers soon.

That Sunday in church, Pastor Rehn preached the Parable of the Talents. Her father nodded once, as if agreeing with his own resolve. Diana watched blue and green light tremble through stained glass. Maybe to go wasn't to abandon—it was to honor what had been given.

After the service, Doreen hooked her arm through Diana's. "Promise you won't get *boring* in college."

"I'll try not to."

"Write me letters."

"I will."

"And don't fall in love with some city boy."

Diana laughed. "No danger of that."

But that night, she imagined what it might be like—to meet someone who didn't already know her stories, who hadn't watched her carry buckets through snow. Someone who could see her as more than a daughter or sister. The thought frightened her, but also opened a small window inside her chest.

By spring, the acceptance letter came. Her father cleared his throat twice before saying, "You'll do well. Just remember where you come from."

She would. But remembering wasn't the same as returning.

That summer, before she left for Madison, she spent a weekend camping with her grandparents at Devil's Lake. It was meant to be simple—fresh air, campfire suppers, the sound of crickets instead of machines. But it became something else entirely. Something she would remember long after she forgot the exact color of the barn.

Chapter 2
The Water's Edge
Courage often arrives disguised as instinct.

The air at Devil's Lake carried the kind of warmth that promised storms by morning.

Grandpa John and Grandma Aleta had pitched the old canvas tent near the tree line, close enough to hear the laughter from the beach but far enough to believe in quiet. Supper had been simple—hot dogs over the fire, peaches from a tin, coffee that smelled faintly of smoke. When the light began to thin, Aleta took out her knitting; John began to hum some tune from the fifties, off-key but content.

Diana stood at the edge of the campsite, watching dusk gather like breath over the hills. She was seventeen, old enough to be trusted and young enough to want to vanish. The lake caught the last of the sun, a long bronze mirror that looked both solid and infinite.

"I'm just going to walk," she said.

"Stay where we can see you," John replied without looking up.

She nodded, already gone.

The path along the shore wound through pines and sandstone. The air smelled of moss and suntan lotion. At the beach, families lingered—children skipping stones, radios murmuring, a lifeguard blowing one last whistle. Diana kept walking. Crowds made her restless; noise interrupted the quiet language she shared with water.

About a quarter mile around the loop, the trees opened to a narrow clearing—a slit of shoreline hidden by sumac and birch. She stepped through the branches and found a small beach no larger than a living room. Two boys were there, maybe six or seven. One stood in the shallows, calling to the other who was farther out, small arms slicing through the dusk-dark surface.

"Come back!" the boy on shore shouted.

The swimmer kept going.

Diana stopped. The wind shifted; the air suddenly colder. She watched the ripples widen, then break unevenly. The boy in the water began to thrash—legs trapped, maybe in weeds, maybe in panic. His head vanished, surfaced, vanished again. The cries from shore turned to sobs.

Without thinking, she dropped her sweatshirt and ran. The sand bit her feet; the water seized her calves with its cold. Then she was swimming—clean strokes, fast, sure. Her body remembered what her mind didn't have time to say.

She reached the boy just as he went under again. His eyes were wide, his mouth full of water. She hooked an arm beneath his chest and kicked hard, pulling him toward the light that marked the shallows. The distance felt longer than it was. For a moment she thought the lake might take them both.

Then her feet found sand. She hauled him up, coughing, gasping, dragging him until he could kneel. The other boy ran to them, still crying. From somewhere up the trail came voices, running feet, a woman's scream.

By the time the mother reached them, Diana was shaking with cold and effort. The woman dropped to her knees, gathering the boy into her arms, her own breath ragged with relief. The rescued child began to sob—loud, wet, alive.

Diana stepped back. Water dripped from her hair onto her arms, tiny rivers of lake and sky. The woman looked up, eyes full, lips parted as if to speak. No words came. She only nodded—a thank-you shaped in silence.

Diana nodded back and turned toward the path.

The walk to camp felt longer in the fading light. Her clothes clung heavy; her skin smelled of algae and metal. She thought of the moment just before she'd jumped—the space between knowing and doing—and wondered what name it had. Later she would call it instinct. Much later, grace.

When she reached the tent, the fire had burned to embers. Aleta looked up, worry turning quickly into relief, then into her grandmother's stern calm.

"Where on earth have you been? We were about to send John looking."

"I—went to the lake. Someone needed help."

Aleta's eyebrows rose. "Help?"

"There was a boy. He couldn't get back in. He's fine now."

Aleta set the knitting aside, studying her for a long moment. Then she smiled—not pride exactly, but recognition.

"You did right," she said softly. "But next time, call for help first."

Diana nodded. The night air smelled of pine and damp wool. Behind her, the lake shimmered faintly under a new moon, silent and enormous. Somewhere out there, a mother was holding her child close, both of them breathing the same borrowed air.

In the dark, Diana felt the world settle again—not unbroken, but balanced enough to hold.

Chapter 3
The Chemistry of Grace
Love is the language we learn before we understand it.

By the time she reached Madison, Diana had learned two things: *that balance was never still, and that grace often arrived disguised as motion.*

The city felt larger than sound itself—bicycles flashing down Bascom Hill, lake wind bending the flags, voices rising from the terrace in a dozen accents. She carried her steadiness like a secret language, the quiet confidence of someone who had already stood at the edge once and chosen to act.

The lake outside her dorm was not Devil's, but it shimmered the same way at dusk—half light, half memory. Sometimes, standing there before class, she would think of that night: the boy's small hand gripping hers, the silence that followed, her grandmother's calm voice by the fire.

She hadn't known it then, but that moment had been a translation—the first of many.

Turning fear into motion. Stillness into meaning.

It was the language she would spend years learning to speak.

Doreen had tucked a note into her jacket: Don't forget us when you become a genius. PS: Remember to eat. She smiled when she found it later that night.

Her dorm smelled faintly of wax and new paint. Her roommate, Jenny from Milwaukee, pinned up Fleetwood Mac posters. "You're from a farm?" she asked.

"Yes."

"That's... kind of cool. You know how to drive a tractor or something?"

"Something like that."

Classes began that Monday. The walk across campus felt like crossing a continent—flyers, laughter, the wind off the lake. She moved within it quietly, like a current under noise.

For three years the seasons turned that way—study, snow, thaw, summer work. By senior year, she had learned how to live alone without feeling lonely. She rented a creaky house on Lathrop Street with three other girls. The city's sound had become her stillness.

Her life had rhythm: coffee at Steep & Brew, tutoring shifts, letters home scented faintly of hay dust. She'd dated a few men—Matt who quoted poets, Chris who wanted marriage, a summer boy who vanished—but none left a mark. She'd learned that affection wasn't always connection.

It was late September of her final year when she first saw Karan.

The Physical Chemistry lecture was crowded, the board a blur of equations. Ten minutes in, the door opened. A man slipped in—dark-haired, coat askew, expression unreadable. He moved with restraint, as if careful not to disturb the air around him.

When he sat, three rows ahead, she noticed his stillness more than his face. He wrote in a looping script that looked foreign, pausing often as if thinking beyond the room.

Their eyes met only once, a brief recognition that felt oddly familiar.

A week later, in the lab, the TA read aloud: "Rao, Karan and Russell, Diana."

He smiled faintly when he reached their bench. "We share initials, it seems."

"Maybe alphabetical inevitability."

He laughed quietly, the sound more breath than voice.

They worked side by side, glass clinking softly. "From India?" she asked.

"Yes. Bombay."

"Long way from here."

"Sometimes distance is the only way to see where you began."

The liquid turned violet. "Beautiful," she murmured.

"That's kinetics," he said. "Or maybe life."

That night she wrote in her notebook: Grace appears not in miracles, but in reactions. Then, No—grace is the reaction.

Years had taught her calm, but his presence disturbed it gently, like a fingertip on still water.

Over the following months, they settled into rhythm—lab work, coffee, walks by the lake. He told her of Bombay's sea; she spoke of barns and frost. "Your world sounds steady," he said.

"It was," she replied.

When winter came, he offered her his scarf outside Observatory Hill. She accepted. They stood above the city lights, breath turning visible in the cold.

"I think you make things seem slower," she said.

"And you make them still."

The kiss that followed felt inevitable and new—the meeting of motion and stillness.

Through that winter and spring they became inseparable, though never loud about it. They studied, shared songs, and borrowed silence. He read her lines from Stevie Wonder songs; she played him a melody that began in repetition and dissolved into open chords.

Even in laughter, she sometimes sensed a distance—as if part of him were already half-turned toward another horizon.

When spring came, magnolias opened all at once. They both knew the year was ending but didn't name it.

One afternoon, by the lake, he asked, "What happens now?"

"Now we wait," she said.

"For what?"

"For whatever comes next."

A week later, at graduation, he found her in the crowd. "Congratulations," he said, handing her a small notebook wrapped in brown paper.

"What's this?"

"Something for you to write in. When you leave, you'll need to keep the center somehow."

"And you?"

"I'll find mine eventually."

On the bus home, she opened it. In his careful handwriting:

Every reaction begins when stillness meets motion.

Chapter 4
The Night of Fire and Silence
Grief reshapes the world without moving a stone.

The night began with sirens.

Not the chasing kind—the shrill, mechanical ones that slice through sleep and thought alike.

Diana was setting the futon in the corner of the Eagle Heights apartment when the hallway erupted in sound. Aai and Baba had arrived that morning; Tai and little Adi were already asleep on borrowed blankets. The room smelled of lentils, detergent, and the faint sweetness of jasmine oil Aai rubbed into her wrists before bed.

"Out! Everyone out!" someone shouted outside.

Karan froze for half a breath, then motioned to Tai. Diana grabbed coats and shoes. They filed down the stairwell—Tai clutching Adi, Aai steadying herself on the rail, Baba moving slowly behind.

In the courtyard, red lights pulsed against the low brick buildings. Snowmelt glistened on the asphalt; students huddled in pajamas and parkas. For a moment the night felt unreal, as if they were watching themselves from a distance.

Karan was counting faces. "Where's Baba?"

She turned—and saw him halfway up the stairs, Aai at his side, one hand gripping the rail. His face looked washed of color. When they reached the courtyard, the alarm cut off. Silence returned too suddenly; it pressed on the ears.

Diana felt the absence of the sound like an aftershock. The only noise left was the wind through the pines.

Inside again, Baba said he was fine—"Just tired, the travel," he insisted, waving away concern. But when he reached for water, the glass trembled in his hand.

By morning, the tremor had become stillness.

They were in the emergency room before dawn. The hallways smelled faintly of antiseptic and coffee. A television murmured news no one watched. Nurses moved with practiced speed; forms appeared, pens scratched, monitors beeped. Diana stood beside Aai, one arm around her shoulders.

Through the half-open door she could see the doctor's hands, precise, urgent; could hear Karan's voice—sharp, frightened, then suddenly quiet.

Time fractured into seconds that refused to pass.

When the doctor stepped out, his eyes said everything before his mouth did.

"Multiple strokes. We've done what we can."

Diana felt Aai's body sag against her. A low sound escaped, not quite a cry. She guided her to a chair. Karan stood motionless, expression emptied. For a moment, she thought he might fall too.

The rest blurred: hospital forms, the priest, the phone calls. She remembered the smell of smoke at the cremation, the faint crackle of wood, the way Aai's fingers refused to unclasp the prayer beads. She remembered Karan's silence most of all—not numbness, but something deeper, an implosion.

They married a week later because everything had already been arranged, and because Aai insisted. "His father wanted this," she said. "The living must honor the living."

The Olbrich botanical gardens felt hollow without him. The lilies smelled too sweet, as if overcompensating. Karan's hands were cold when he placed the ring on hers. She whispered the vow—*I promise to hold the center, even when edges pull*—and felt the words land heavier than she expected.

That night, when guests had gone and the candles were out, she found him sitting by the window, still in his wedding clothes, staring at the snow. "You should sleep," she said gently.

He didn't answer.

Only after a long pause did he murmur, "Everything's still burning, even when it looks like ash."

She knelt beside him, resting her head against his shoulder. "Then let it burn," she whispered. "We'll rebuild from what's left."

But he didn't turn toward her.

In the weeks that followed, he spoke through motion—packing boxes, filling out job applications, defending his dissertation with mechanical perfection. Action as anesthesia. People called it strength; she recognized it as survival.

Diana's own thesis defense came two months later. She rehearsed in the quiet hours while he slept on the couch, papers spread like snowdrifts around him. When the day arrived, he sat in the back row, eyes shadowed but smiling.

"You did beautifully," he said afterward, voice flat with exhaustion.

"I wish you'd been listening," she almost said, but didn't.

They moved to Austin, Minnesota, that spring. She accepted a position at a food company—steady pay, health insurance, a promise of order.

The road north was lined with melting snow and open fields. In the passenger seat, Karan watched the horizon as if searching for an answer. Diana drove, one hand steady on the wheel, the other resting lightly on his notebook between them.

Inside it, she knew, were pages of equations and questions that might never be resolved.

She thought again of her own definition of translation: turning code into function, thought into life.

Outside, the sky cleared. For a moment she imagined the center holding—not unbroken, but intact enough to begin again.

Chapter 5
The Quiet Equations
Some silences are calculations waiting for truth.

Austin was perfect, as she expected—a grid of quiet streets, grain elevators, and the faint, sweet smell of pork drifting from the Hormel plant.

They arrived in April. The last snow was melting, leaving the ground slick with mud and the air heavy with thaw. The neighbors waved politely and went back to mowing. Inside, boxes waited to be opened, but neither of them moved quickly.

Karan stood by the window, staring out at the gray water.

"Different kind of silence here," he said.

"Better or worse?"

"Just different."

Diana set up the kitchen first—plates, cups, the quilted potholders her mother had sewn into a housewarming gift. She liked order; it was her language for care. He helped for a while, then disappeared into the spare bedroom that would become his office.

At the food company, her days began at six-forty-five. White coats, stainless-steel counters, the hum of steam retorts. The work was exacting and strangely peaceful: measuring protein content in samples, logging data, writing small reports that no one outside the lab would ever read. She liked the precision. Numbers stayed honest; they didn't withdraw.

Evenings were longer. Sometimes Karan cooked elaborate curries that perfumed the air for days; sometimes he skipped dinner entirely, lost in the pale light of his computer. She learned to read his silences—there were the mild ones, when he was thinking, and the deeper ones, when thinking had turned into disappearance.

Letters came from her parents—questions about insurance, weather, whether the town had a church "with decent music." Doreen sent postcards from her own classroom in Madison: *My students think I'm ancient at twenty-two. Tell Karan to smile sometimes.*

Diana smiled reading them but didn't show him.

Summer brought lilacs and long twilights. She planted herbs in tin cans on the windowsill; he built a small desk out of pine. They attended a few dinners with colleagues—polite talk, paper plates, the clink of wineglasses. Karan spoke little but listened intently, as if translating every sentence into another tongue before understanding it.

When they walked home, she would slip her arm through his. Sometimes he leaned closer; other times his body seemed made of distance.

One night in July, thunder rolled low over the fields. Power flickered, and the house fell into shadow. She found him in the office, staring at his notebook.

"You're still awake," she said.

"I couldn't stop."

"From what?"

"Thinking how everything decays. Even equations."

She touched his shoulder. "You're allowed to rest."

He smiled without warmth. "You rest for both of us."

Later, in bed, she listened to the rain tapping the roof and wondered what it meant to keep loving someone who was slowly slipping into his own gravity.

Chapter 6
The Distance Between
Even gentle hearts can bruise against the world.

The morning they went to the bank, the air already smelled like new beginnings—fresh coffee, thawed earth, the faint metallic promise of spring.

They had been house-hunting for weeks, circling listings in the *Austin Daily Herald*, driving past picket fences and budding maples, imagining which one would hold their future. For once, both were buoyant—two professionals with good salaries, steady credit, and the audacity of shared plans.

"Front porch," Karan said, tapping the photo of a white-clapboard house. "I could read there every morning."

"And I could plant basil in the window boxes," Diana added.

They smiled, building a castle out of ordinary dreams.

On the way to the bank they stopped at a small diner off Main Street. The sign said *Mabel's Kitchen—Homemade Since 1954.* Inside, the booths were red vinyl, the air thick with coffee and bacon grease. A waitress with a beehive bun dropped menus on the table.

They ordered meatloaf and iced tea, laughed about paint colors, and talked about mortgage rates as if they were secret codes to happiness. It felt easy, almost weightless—until the check arrived.

The waitress returned, pen poised. Her tone carried something that wasn't curiosity.

"Is this going to be together or separate?"

Diana's hand was in Karan's. He looked up, surprised. "Together, please."

The woman's eyes flicked from him to Diana, then back again. "Are you sure?"

The words landed like grit on glass. Karan nodded, still polite, but his shoulders stiffened.

The waitress hesitated before leaving the bill. When she did, she set it closer to Diana.

They finished quietly. On the way to the car, Karan smiled, but it was the practiced kind—the one that hides the bruise before it forms. The drive that followed was silent except for the turn signal clicking like a metronome between them.

Outside the bank, Diana's phone rang—Doreen.

"Take it," Karan said gently. "I'll start the paperwork."

She hesitated, but Doreen never called just once. "I won't be long."

The conversation—lesson plans, a new student, the price of gas—unspooled longer than she meant. When she finally hung up, twenty minutes had passed.

Inside the bank, fluorescent lights buzzed. A receptionist glanced up, uncertain. Diana spotted Karan sitting alone on a lobby chair, hands clasped, staring at a wall as if it had spoken something he couldn't answer.

Before she could reach him, a man in a gray suit intercepted her.

"Ma'am, excuse me—are you with this gentleman?"

"Yes," she said. "My husband."

The man's expression flickered—authority turning to apology, then back to control.

"He came in saying that. We—uh—had some concerns. He presented identification, and said you were outside. One of our tellers thought he might be… impersonating someone. We were about to call the police."

Diana blinked. "You were what?"

The manager's voice softened but stayed defensive. "It's just protocol, you understand. Something didn't match in the system."

"He's my husband," she said again, slower this time, as if repetition might restore gravity. "We're applying for a home loan. Together."

The man's face flushed. "Of course. My apologies. I'll... let them know."

He disappeared behind the counter.

Diana crossed the room and sat beside Karan. He didn't look at her. His jaw was set, his hands still. She took one, and he let her, but the warmth was gone.

They finished the paperwork in silence. The manager returned once with perfunctory politeness, offering coffee neither of them touched.

Outside, the sky had turned gray. They walked to the car without speaking. The only sound was the crunch of gravel underfoot.

At dinner that night, neither mentioned the diner or the bank. She made pasta; he poured wine. The radio played something soft. When the meal ended, he cleared the plates, rinsed them carefully, and left them to dry without a word.

That night the house was quiet, the kind of quiet that hums beneath thought.

Diana washed the dishes while Karan read by the window, the lamplight cutting his face into planes of gold and shadow.

No apology came, no conversation followed—only the faint clink of plates, the slow rhythm of water over porcelain.

In that silence she sensed a new variable between them, small but precise, the kind that alters every equation afterward.

Later, in bed, Diana lay awake listening to the wind against the eaves. The world had tilted slightly, not enough to fall, just enough to notice.

By morning, life would resume its ordinary order, but the world had shifted by an inch—just enough to feel the weight of it.

Chapter 7
The Laws of Stillness
Distance grows slowly, like winter on a window.

By autumn, the tilt had become a rhythm.

Life resumed its careful order—work, meals, weekends measured by grocery lists and the changing color of fields. Yet something invisible had settled between them, a silence that wasn't an absence so much as pressure.

Her first-year review at the food company was solid; her supervisor called her "steady, detail-oriented." The word *steady made* her both proud and tired. She left work at four, stopped at Hy-Vee for groceries, and drove home past fields already turning amber.

He was on the porch when she pulled in, sitting cross-legged with a mug of tea gone cold.

"Long day?" she asked.

He nodded, eyes on the horizon. "I miss the ocean."

"The nearest one's a thousand miles away."

"I know. That's why I miss it."

She wanted to ask what he saw when he looked that far, but the question felt too sharp. Instead, she sat beside him. The air smelled of cut grass and diesel.

"Remember Madison?" she said finally. "All those mornings by the lake?"

"I remember the fog," he said. "You couldn't see where the water ended."

"That's what I miss—the not-knowing."

For the first time in months he laughed, softly. "You've become a poet."

"Maybe *you* left the language behind for me to find."

He turned toward her then, eyes tired but alive, and for a moment the distance folded.

Winter came early again. Frost climbed the windows; the river froze in slow sheets. Diana learned the rhythm of small-town life—weekend markets, potlucks, the kindness of strangers who remembered names. Karan grew thinner, quieter. He started walking late at night, saying the cold helped him think.

Sometimes she woke to the sound of the door closing softly. She would wait, listening for his return, imagining the snow lighting the sidewalks around him.

She didn't tell anyone. To the world they were fine—young professionals, new homeowners, polite smiles. Inside, they orbited each other carefully, two celestial bodies held by memory rather than gravity.

On New Year's Eve, she baked a pie and set two forks beside it. He came home just before midnight, cheeks red from the cold.

"You should have come," he said. "The sky was clear. You could see everything."

"I can see enough from here."

He looked at her then—really looked, as if surprised she was still there.

"You keep the lights on," he said softly.

"That's what the center does," she answered.

The company cafeteria smelled faintly of yeast and chlorine. Diana sat by the window with her lunch tray—vegetable soup, an apple, a cup of black coffee—watching trucks back up to the loading dock below. The rhythm of work suited her: the measured whir of machines, the low conversation of coworkers, the predictable comfort of schedules. She liked the small satisfactions—a process improved, a shipment released on time. Order could be tender, she had learned, if you treated it that way.

Karan's days were less defined. The University's satellite research center in Austin occupied a renovated building near the river, a cluster of glass offices and old brick labs. His fellowship focused on predictive modeling—applying theoretical frameworks to biological systems. When he tried to explain, his words folded in on themselves.

"It's all a reaction," he said once. "Trying to understand why things behave when they shouldn't."

She smiled. "You mean people?"

"Sometimes."

They drove in together most mornings, splitting at the intersection where the road forked toward the University on one side and the plant on the other. He always turned left first. She waved, even when he didn't look back.

Evenings came quietly. They ate dinner on the small deck behind their house—Dal (Indian soup) and rice, a bottle of local wine, and conversation that drifted toward the ordinary. Bills, recipes, the neighbor's new dog. He still laughed easily, but less often. When he did, it sounded like a memory.

In winter, she bought a lamp that mimicked daylight and kept it on the counter. He called it *"the sun-in-a-box."*

"Everything's too bright here already," he teased.

"Then we're even," she said. "You bring the dark."

He looked up sharply, surprised by the accuracy, then smiled as if forgiving her for it.

On weekends they sometimes drove north to Rochester to see friends from Madison. Conversation always turned to work—promotions, research grants, mortgage rates. Diana noticed how other couples touched each other absent-mindedly, hands brushing, shoulders leaning. She and Karan sat with space between them—not discomfort exactly, but absence of reflex.

Once, on the drive home, she asked, "Do you ever think about what comes next?"

"Next?"

"After all this. The work, the papers."

He considered it for a long time. "I used to think about the future. Now I mostly think about meaning."

"Isn't that the same thing?"

"Maybe. But meaning moves slower and in a roundabout way."

She wanted to ask if she was part of that meaning, but the question stayed unspoken, coiled somewhere in her throat.

The fellowship was to end in six months. He was offered an extension, he was not sure.

"I need time to think," he said.

She almost laughed. "You always need time to think."

He didn't answer, and she regretted the words instantly.

At the food company, her supervisor offered her a promotion—Assistant Manager of Research Operations. It meant more pay, longer hours, a small office with a window that faced the loading bay. She accepted. She needed the structure, the promise that something was still moving forward.

That summer, the house filled with heat. They bought a second fan instead of an air conditioner. Karan started spending afternoons at the library. When she asked what he was working on, he said, "A proposal. Or maybe a confession. I haven't decided which."

At night she heard him typing. The sound used to comfort her. Now it made her feel like a guest in her own life.

One evening she came home to find him on the porch again, staring at the horizon as if waiting for something to materialize.

"You should eat," she said.

"Not hungry."

"You've barely eaten all week."

He nodded absently. "I keep thinking of Baba."

She sat beside him. "Grief isn't a project, Karan."

"No. It's an equation without balance."

He said it gently, but she felt the distance in it—the way he could turn pain into abstraction faster than she could name it.

Inside, the dinner grew cold.

Late that fall, she found a notebook on his desk, open to a page filled with fragments: *hollow, horizon, silence, recursion.*

In the margin he had written, *When translation fails, meaning fractures.*

She touched the words lightly, then closed the book. On her way out, she turned off the desk lamp.

That night, as she lay in bed, the wind rattled the window like a heartbeat out of rhythm. She turned toward his side, empty again. Through the crack under the door, a thin strip of light spilled from the study.

She didn't cry.

Grace, she realized, wasn't always gentle—it was the discipline of staying.

When he finally came to bed, she pretended to be asleep. He lay on his back, staring at the ceiling. After a long time, he whispered something she almost didn't catch.

"I keep hearing him, you know. Baba (Karan's father)."

She kept her eyes closed. "What does he say?"

"Nothing. That's the worst part."

She waited until his breathing steadied before turning toward him. His hand had fallen across the quilt her mother had made—the same quilt that had covered their wedding bed, stitched from old dresses. She placed her hand over his, softly, careful not to wake him.

Outside, snow began to fall again, covering the streetlights, softening the world to silence.

She lay awake, listening, until the edges of night began to lighten. Somewhere deep inside her, something shifted—not a break, but the quiet recognition that grace might no longer mean holding still.

Chapter 8
The Crossing
To enter another world is to remember your own.

When Diana first said she wanted to go to India, Karan looked at her for a long time before answering.

"Are you sure?" he asked.

"Yes," she said. "It's time, just the two of us, it will be fun."

The trip began before sunrise—Minneapolis still asleep under a gray sheet of snow. At the airport, she watched other travelers line up with carts piled high with luggage, bright tags marked *BOM*. There was a different kind of anticipation in the air: not vacation, but return.

Delta 164, Minneapolis to Amsterdam. The flight attendants smiled in practiced rhythm, meals came and went, and hours folded into themselves. Over the Atlantic, Karan slept with his hand lightly touching hers, the kind of half-sleep that only comes from long anticipation. She looked out the window at the cloud fields below, thinking how strange it was to be carried halfway across the world by motion she couldn't feel.

At Schiphol, they wandered the concourse in a daze—Dutch tulips, stroopwafels, a soft drizzle beyond the glass. Then another boarding call: Mumbai. The names on the loudspeakers shifted from Dutch to English, and something in Karan's face softened, like a chord resolving.

The first thing she noticed on landing was the air.

Heavy, warm, alive. A thousand smells colliding—diesel, jasmine, sweat, salt.

And then came the sound: a roar of voices, horns, announcements, laughter.

At the arrivals gate, a small crowd waved frantically: aunts, uncles, cousins, faces glowing with familiarity. Aai was there, sari perfectly pleated despite the humidity; Tai, radiant, holding a garland; and behind them, three more relatives Diana couldn't yet place.

"Karan!" they shouted. "Karan's come home!"

He bent to touch their feet, one by one, murmuring "Namaskar" each time.

When he reached Aai, she placed her hand on his head and whispered a blessing that Diana didn't understand but felt in her chest.

The next two days in Mumbai passed in a blur of love and noise.

They stayed in his aunt's Andheri flat—narrow hallways, tiled floors, a ceiling fan that whirred like a heartbeat. Meals appeared endlessly: puris puffed like balloons, dal shimmering with ghee, fish curry fragrant with kokum (Indian spice). Every few hours, new guests arrived, bearing sweets and stories.

At night they gathered on the rooftop terrace under strings of yellow bulbs. Philosophy and gossip mingled freely—Marathi, English, Hindi weaving in and out of one another. Laughter rose like music. Someone passed around chai in steel tumblers; someone else began to sing an old Kishore Kumar song. Diana sat cross-legged beside Aai, her hands wrapped around the warm cup, smiling at a world that seemed built on generosity.

On the third morning, they packed for the drive to Belgaum.

Aai insisted on joining, along with Tai and the driver, Imran—a gentle man with a quick smile and an unwavering horn. Diana started in the front seat to ward off motion sickness, but after twenty kilometers of Mumbai traffic, she asked to switch. "Too close to the madness," she said, laughing, and climbed into the back beside Karan.

The road south unfurled through plains and sugarcane fields, every mile layered with color and dust. Vendors sold coconuts from roadside carts; herds of goats blocked the way; temple bells rang faintly from passing villages. The air changed as they crossed into the Deccan plateau—drier, spiced with earth and smoke.

They stopped in Sangli for lunch with Tai and her husband, Bhau. Like so many in Karan's family, both were doctors—real ones, Diana noted, the kind who healed people instead of analyzing data. Bhau's clinic stood next to their home, and patients still trickled in even as the family gathered for tea. "It never stops," Tai said, laughing, "but that's life."

By the time they reached Belgaum, dusk had softened the horizon.

The family home rose like something out of another century—arched verandas, high ceilings, faded shutters the color of monsoon sky. The plaster had peeled in places, ivy climbing the walls like memory itself. And in the center of it all stood **Sudha**, Karan's grandmother—small, upright, eyes sharp as sunlight.

"She was the sun," Karan whispered as they approached. "We all orbit her."

When Sudha spoke, her voice carried both command and warmth. "So this is Diana," she said, taking her hands. "Finally."

They connected instantly—first over stories, then over yoga. Diana admitted she dabbled; Sudha smiled, "Then you already understand. The body remembers what the soul forgets."

The days that followed felt timeless.

Visitors came and went in steady waves—relatives, neighbors, childhood friends of Karan's father, each bringing food or questions or blessings. Every evening turned into a celebration: platters of biryani, bowls of curries that glowed gold and red, children darting between the tables. Diana tried to keep track of names but finally gave up.

"Five hundred," Karan joked one night, grinning. "You've met about five hundred people now. That's half my family."

When the house grew quiet at night, they would sit on the veranda, listening to crickets and distant temple bells. For the first time in years, she saw Karan unguarded. His laughter—loud, uncalculated—rolled through the courtyard like wind.

After a week, they drove west to Goa to visit the shrines and the sea.

Karan's uncle owned a small beach resort there—simple cottages under palm trees, the ocean humming just beyond the dunes. Mornings began with chai on the porch, afternoons with fish grilled straight from the surf. Diana walked the shoreline at dusk, toes sinking into wet sand, watching Karan chase waves with the same boyish energy she had only glimpsed in stories.

One evening, she caught him standing ankle-deep in the tide, arms open to the wind, laughing at something only the sea could answer. The light caught his face, and she thought: *This is what he looked like before the weight came.*

They stayed three more days before flying home—Goa to Mumbai, Mumbai to Paris, Paris to Minneapolis. The return felt impossibly long in hours but short in feeling, as if the journey had folded back on itself.

On the plane, Karan fell asleep again, his hand resting over hers. She looked out at the clouds—bright white, endless—and thought about all that motion contained inside stillness. For the first time in years, she wasn't holding the center alone.

For a moment, she let herself believe that grace could also mean joy.

Chapter 9
Leaving the Lattice
Purpose bends as quietly as light.

The snow began before they landed.

A soft, drifting veil over the Minneapolis lights — delicate, endless, indifferent.

After weeks of color and sound, the silence of it felt unreal.

At baggage claim, Karan stood still for a long moment, watching flakes melt against the glass.

"Everything's too quiet," he said.

Diana smiled faintly. "That's what home sounds like."

But in that pause she sensed what he did not say: *not this home.*

The house in Austin felt hollow after India.

Even the air was too clean, stripped of scent. The suitcase by the door still carried traces of turmeric and sandalwood.

When Diana opened it, she found one of Aai's bangles tangled in a scarf. She held it to her ear — a faint metallic chime, a heartbeat from another world.

For a while, Karan seemed lighter.

He wrote long emails to his mother, even called his sister.

But within weeks, the brightness faded.

He buried himself in the lab again, chasing precision the way others chase prayer. His office at the University of Minnesota satellite campus in Austin was spotless — glassware aligned, equations sharp on the board, everything under control except himself.

He came home later each night, his words clipped shorter, his silences longer.

Diana tried to understand the language of that weariness.

He had told her once that research was discovery; now he said it was performance.

Every grant proposal became a theater of persuasion.

Every experiment bent toward what the sponsors wanted to see.

"You don't research the truth," he said one night, not looking up from his notes. "You research permission."

She wanted to tell him he was still building meaning — but meaning, for him, had to be pure. Anything less felt like betrayal.

At work, her own world remained steady.

The food company had grown; her responsibilities had too.

She liked the tangible simplicity of it — numbers that matched outcomes, formulas that became food. It grounded her.

Karan called it "chemical pragmatism."

She called it peace.

Karan leaned back against the wall and said, "Maybe this is how life repairs itself — quietly, without permission."

She nodded, though she wasn't sure he believed it.

At the university, the months blurred:

Two new papers, two rejected grants.

A colleague was promoted for politics, not merit.

Karan smiled through the congratulations, came home early, and stared out the window as snow began to fall again.

The next morning he told her he was leaving academia.

They were sitting at the kitchen table — tea between them, the maple tree bare outside.

"I think I'm done chasing papers," he said.

She looked up slowly. "You mean for good?"

He nodded. "The lattice doesn't lead anywhere. It just circles itself."

"What will you do instead?"

He smiled — brittle, almost a laugh. "Something real. Something I can touch. Maybe just breathe for a while."

A week later, he met Richard, a manager from a local food company — rough hands, clear eyes, the kind of man who spoke without theater.

Karan told Diana later that at the end of their meeting, Richard said, "You'll get your hands dirty here. Are you okay with that?"

When he came home that evening, there was snow on his coat and a quiet in his voice that she hadn't heard before.

"From equations to emulsions," he said, half to himself.

Diana smiled. "From grants to groceries."

He laughed — real laughter, brief but alive.

And she thought, *Maybe this is what healing sounds like.*

But later that night, as she washed the tea cups, she saw him at the window again, staring at nothing.

Outside, the snow was falling in clean, endless silence.

Inside, she felt the first edge of distance return — faint but familiar.

He was stepping into the real world at last.

She only hoped he would remember how to stay.

Chapter 10
House of Small Wonders
Joy builds its home in the softest spaces.

The house that once echoed with theory now smelled of milk and soap.

Morning light filtered through the curtains, softened by the thin frost on the window. The maple outside had turned its first gold, and in the bassinet by the couch, a small sound—half-sigh, half-dream—rose and fell like breathing made visible.

Anya.

Even her name felt round, vowel-soft and complete.

Diana leaned over, tracing a fingertip along her daughter's cheek. Skin so new it reflected light. The baby's hand opened and closed around nothing, as if catching pieces of the world before they disappeared.

Karan stood behind her, still in the shirt he'd worn to the plant the day before. "She has your nose," he said.

Diana smiled. "And your stubborn chin."

He laughed, quiet so he wouldn't wake her. It was the first true laughter she'd heard from him in months.

Those early weeks blurred—feedings, laundry, lists stuck to the fridge with magnets. Sleep came in fragments; time lost its edges. The black dog stayed away then. Even Karan seemed lighter, as if the universe had granted them a reprieve.

He came home smelling of spice and steel, stories of valves and formulas tucked between his fingers. "They let me build the new process from scratch," he told her once. "No committees. Just hands and ideas."

"That's what you wanted," she said.

He nodded. "It's different when it's real."

On Sundays they walked to the park by the river. Karan pushed the stroller, humming tunelessly, while Diana collected leaves for the scrapbook she would never finish.

The air smelled of grass and diesel, life and machinery intertwined.

Sometimes they stopped for coffee at the diner near Main Street—the same one where the waitress once questioned them. The memory lingered like a scar, but routine had covered it. Now the waitress smiled automatically, calling Anya "sweet pea." Diana took that small civility as victory enough.

Winter folded around them. Snow stacked high against the porch rail; the world shrank to the radius of what they could reach. In that smallness, life found rhythm.

Karan shoveled; Diana baked.

At night, when Anya finally slept, they sat by the heater with mugs of tea, reading in companionable silence. She noticed how the lines in his face softened when the house grew quiet.

"This feels almost holy," he said once.

"What does?"

"Ordinary peace."

She wanted to tell him it had always been holy—he'd just never stayed still long enough to see it.

By spring she was pregnant again.

The news arrived like a secret too delicate to announce. She told him on a Thursday evening, halfway through making dinner. He looked at her, eyes wide, then knelt, pressing his forehead against her stomach as if listening for a sound that didn't yet exist.

"Another small wonder," he whispered.

Mira was born on a September night.

Lightning in the distance, nurses moving briskly, the scent of antiseptic mingled with rain. Karan held her first—awkwardly, reverently—and Diana thought she'd never seen him look so unguarded.

Two daughters.

Two tiny proofs that the universe still bent toward continuation.

Life grew denser.

The living room filled with toys, the refrigerator with magnets and crayon drawings. The house smelled perpetually of oatmeal, detergent, and crayons. Mornings began with cartoons and ended with lullabies; between them lay entire lifetimes of spilled juice and laughter.

Karan went to night school for business courses—an idea that seemed both impulsive and inevitable.

"If I'm going to build something, I should learn how to keep it alive," he said.

Diana encouraged him, though she noticed the fatigue under his enthusiasm. He worked eight hours at the plant, three more in class, and still rose for midnight feedings without complaint.

Sometimes she woke to find him standing by the crib, watching both girls sleep.

"What are you thinking?" she asked once.

"That they don't know how lucky they make us," he said.

Her own world expanded in quieter ways. She joined a mothers' group, learned the small diplomacy of playgrounds and pediatric appointments. At work, she shifted to part-time; her supervisor called her "balanced," which she accepted as both compliment and concession.

Evenings belonged to the four of them: dinners that ended in laughter, baths that became splash wars, storybooks read until everyone fell asleep mid-sentence.

On Saturdays, they drove out to the countryside, showing the girls the world in pieces: apple orchards, county fairs, the blue curve of the horizon.

Anya asked endless questions; Mira watched in silence, eyes absorbing everything.

"They're opposite forces," Karan said. "Curiosity and contemplation."

"Like their parents," she teased.

He smiled. "Let's hope they inherit the better halves."

One autumn afternoon, Diana came home to find the kitchen transformed.

Paper cranes hung from the light fixture; construction-paper stars lined the cabinets. Karan stood at the stove wearing one of her aprons, flour on his cheek.

"Surprise," he said. "Anya helped."

"What's the occasion?"

"Nothing. That's the point."

She looked around the room—the mess, the laughter—and thought, *This is what grace looks like when it forgets it's holy.*

Years blurred gently.

Photographs filled frames: first steps, birthday cakes, trips to the zoo. The girls grew taller; the house grew smaller. The maple outside spread wider each year, its shade deepening over the porch.

Sometimes, late at night, Diana would step outside and listen—the hum of crickets, the faint rumble of a distant train—and realize that happiness had become less an event and more a temperature, something constant but invisible.

One winter morning, Karan left early for the plant, and she found a note on the counter:

For all that we've built, and all we still can. —K.

She pinned it to the fridge beside Anya's drawing of a stick-figure family holding hands under a sun too large for the sky.

That evening, as she tucked the girls into bed, Anya asked, "Mom, what's grace?"

Diana hesitated, thinking of all the meanings that word had carried.

Finally she said, "It's what happens when love keeps working, even when you're tired."

Anya considered this seriously, then nodded. "Like you and Dad."

Diana kissed her forehead. "Exactly."

When she turned off the light, the room glowed faintly from the night-lamp—a soft halo over the two small beds. She stood in the doorway, listening to their breathing, the house settling, the slow pulse of her own heart.

Outside, snow began to fall again—quiet, clean, endless.

She thought of all the worlds she'd left and all the ones she'd built.

For the first time in years, she felt no need to choose between them.

The center held.

The rhythm of their life became so complete that it almost disappeared into itself.

Days followed one another like beads on a string—work, school, meals, laughter, sleep.

Grace, Diana thought, wasn't dramatic; it was repetition done with love.

Karan's schedule grew heavier but purposeful. He finished his night classes, framed the certificate, and hung it

51

crookedly in the hallway. "Proof of survival," he said, smiling.

At the plant, his projects expanded. He began designing new formulations—nutrient blends, emulsifiers, things that turned raw material into food with structure and shelf life. "Chemistry with consequence," he liked to call it.

Some evenings he came home glowing with energy, describing an experiment that had worked or a line worker who'd told him he wasn't like the other engineers. Other nights he sat at the kitchen table long after the dishes were done, sketching equations on napkins, his tea going cold.

Diana learned to read those silences too. They weren't absences yet—just the mind turning too fast to rest.

The girls thrived.

Anya, five, asked questions faster than Diana could answer them. "Why does snow squeak? How do people know what time it is without clocks? Why are there no stars in the daytime?"

Mira, three, was quieter, more deliberate. She drew circles again and again on scrap paper, each one a little more perfect than the last. When Diana asked what they were, she said, "Homes for the stars when they get tired."

Weekends were their world.

Saturday pancakes, Anya helping stir the batter; Sunday drives to the farmer's market where Mira clutched a bag of apples as if they were treasure. Diana watched Karan lift the girls onto his shoulders, laughing as they squealed, his voice mixing with theirs—loud, bright, unguarded.

There were moments she wished she could bottle, to save for darker times she didn't yet know were coming.

One summer, they built a swing in the backyard.

Karan drew the design on a napkin, just like his equations. Diana sanded the wood smooth, the girls painted it unevenly, and when it was done, he tested it himself—his long legs kicking the air like a boy's.

That evening they sat on the porch, watching the girls take turns under the maple's shade.

"Do you ever feel like we've finally learned the rhythm?" she asked.

He looked at her, a half-smile forming. "For now. But life's tempo always changes."

She laughed. "Then we'll just keep time together."

He nodded, but his gaze drifted toward the horizon, where the sun was slipping behind the grain elevators.

Autumn came again—golden leaves, cool mornings, the smell of baked apples.

Karan took on a new role at the plant, part management, part research. It paid well but demanded more.

He left before sunrise, returned after dusk. His laughter thinned, replaced by an exhaustion that words couldn't fix.

Still, when he walked in the door, the girls ran to him, and for those few minutes, the world reset.

Diana began practicing yoga again, just ten minutes before dawn.

It started as a way to ease her back pain, but something in the stillness drew her deeper.

Each morning she unrolled the mat quietly, moving between breaths as the house slept.

Balance, stretch, surrender. The motions became prayer, though she never called them that.

One day, Karan woke early and watched her from the doorway.

"You make stillness look like work," he said.

She smiled without stopping. "It is work."

He watched for a moment longer, then said softly, "Maybe I should learn that."

She wanted to tell him he already knew how—he'd just forgotten—but the words stayed unspoken.

By winter, small cracks began to show.

At dinner, he was distracted, sometimes irritable. The girls sensed it, tiptoeing around his moods with the intuition children have for storms.

When Diana asked what was wrong, he said, "Just tired. Too many moving parts."

But later, she found him awake at two a.m., sitting in the dark kitchen, staring into his cup of tea as if the surface might answer him.

He smiled when she entered, but it was the wrong kind of smile—tight, rehearsed.

"Go back to bed," he said gently.

She did, though sleep never came.

Spring returned, and with it, a brief reprieve.

Karan's new process won an award from the company; a photo of him shaking hands with the regional manager appeared in the local paper. The girls pasted it into their scrapbook under the heading *Daddy Builds Food*.

He laughed when he saw it, real laughter that filled the room.

For a while, that sound returned often enough to make her believe the worst had passed.

But Diana had begun to notice something else.

When he came home, he opened a beer before taking off his coat. Just one, always one, though the fridge held more.

At first it seemed harmless—ritual, not escape.

Then one beer became two, the rhythm of his evenings slowly shifting.

She said nothing. Not out of fear, but because silence sometimes felt kinder than confrontation.

The girls grew, and so did their lives.

Anya started kindergarten; Mira discovered music.

Diana went back to full-time work, balancing spreadsheets and science reports while keeping the household orbit steady.

She marveled at how joy persisted—not as grand declarations, but as small mercies: a new drawing on the fridge, the smell of soup on a cold day, the warmth of Karan's hand reaching for hers, even when words failed.

On Anya's seventh birthday, they threw a party in the backyard.

Neighbors, colleagues, laughter spilling over the fence.

Karan grilled skewers, the girls ran barefoot through the grass, the air smelled of smoke and frosting.

At dusk, when the guests left and the children slept, Diana found him sitting alone by the swing, staring at the darkening sky.

"You did well," she said, placing a hand on his shoulder.

He looked up. "They make it easy."

"Then why do you look so far away?"

He hesitated, then shook his head. "I don't know. Sometimes I feel like I'm living two lives—one that everyone sees and one that's just... noise."

She sat beside him, not answering.

The night was still, the kind of stillness that carries both peace and warning.

In the weeks that followed, he began taking long walks after dinner.

"Just clearing my head," he'd say, kissing her cheek, returning an hour later smelling faintly of cold air and solitude.

The girls waited for his footsteps before sleeping.

Diana waited too, counting them in her head like beads on a string.

One evening he came home with a small bottle of whiskey. "A gift from a coworker," he said. "Just for weekends."

She nodded, though her stomach tightened.

The bottle lasted longer than she expected, but the silence that followed each glass lingered even longer.

Summer approached again.

From the outside, their life looked perfect—two bright daughters, good jobs, a house that glowed warm from within.

But Diana knew perfection was often just patience stretched thin.

She began to hold her yoga poses a little longer each morning, steadying her breath as if anchoring the whole house with it.

One morning, as sunlight spilled across the kitchen, she watched Karan tie his shoes for work.

He looked up, catching her gaze.

"What?" he asked, half-smiling.

"Nothing," she said. "Just... grateful."

He stood, kissed her forehead, and left.

The door closed softly behind him.

She turned toward the window, exhaling.

In the yard, the swing moved on its own, slow and soundless in the breeze.

The center held—but she could feel the wind beginning to rise.

Chapter 11
Under the Frost
What cracks in darkness can bloom in dawn.

The breakdown didn't arrive like thunder.

It arrived like frost—slowly, invisibly, and everywhere at once.

To anyone looking in, Karan's life gleamed with order.

A stable career.

A house that smelled faintly of coffee and crayons.

A wife whose steadiness was legendary.

Two daughters whose laughter could lift the dullest morning.

The neighbors waved; the coworkers envied; even Diana's parents said, "You both make it look easy."

But ease, she had learned, could be a kind of camouflage.

It started with small omissions: the way he forgot to shave, or how the mail piled up on his desk unopened.

At dinner, he would drift mid-sentence, eyes far away, as though listening to some frequency only he could hear.

She recognized the signs—not of fatigue but of retreat.

A man vanishing from the inside out.

He still made pancakes on Sundays, still read to the girls, still smiled when neighbors passed, but something in him had gone dim.

Diana could feel it even when he wasn't in the room, like a shadow changing the temperature of the house.

At night he lay awake, the glow of his phone lighting the ceiling.

When she asked what kept him up, he said, "Just thinking."

But the word sounded foreign on his tongue, stripped of curiosity.

She sometimes caught him staring at the wall, unmoving, his face empty of expression.

"Papa?" the girls would ask, tugging his sleeve.

He'd blink and return to them, forcing a smile that never quite reached his eyes.

The black dog had returned—not barking, not snarling, just waiting.

It followed him to meetings, rode shotgun on long commutes, curled beside him when the world went silent.

He never spoke its name, but Diana saw the leash dragging behind.

He began staying later at work.

"Deadlines," he'd say.

But the deadlines were endless, shifting just enough to excuse absence.

Some evenings she'd call, and he wouldn't answer; then the text would come—"Heading back soon. Don't wait up."

The smell of whiskey arrived before the explanation.

Not heavy, not daily—just enough to dull the edges.

He still functioned, still performed, but Diana sensed the drink wasn't about pleasure.

It was anesthesia, disguised as habit.

She didn't call it alcoholism. The word felt too simple, too mechanical for what she saw.

This wasn't thirst; it was ache.

A hole in the soul trying to remember what it felt like to be whole.

One night she found him sitting in the dark kitchen, glass in hand, untouched.

"You all right?" she asked.

He shrugged. "Just tired."

"Tired of what?"

He thought for a long time before answering.

"Of trying to be fine."

She wanted to reach across the table, to touch his hand, but something in his stillness warned her: don't move too fast or it will vanish.

So she stayed, silent beside him, until the first light crept into the room.

The decline gathered momentum in quiet increments.

He ate less. Smiled less. Spoke less.

The girls tiptoed around him, sensing the fragility adults call *a mood*.

When he was home, he floated between rooms like a ghost still loyal to the living.

Then came the morning when he didn't get out of bed.

"Just today," he murmured. "Headache."

Diana called in sick for him, then for herself.

By evening he was still staring at the ceiling, pupils wide, hands folded on his chest as though bracing for impact.

She drove him to the clinic the next morning.

Ten days, the doctor said gently.

A short stay. Observation. Rest.

Generose Unit, part of Mayo.

He didn't resist. Agreement had become his last form of control.

The ward was bright, neutral, and heartbreakingly calm.

No chaos, no screams—just quiet corridors and the sound of pages turning.

When she left him that first night, he looked both relieved and ashamed, like a man who'd finally confessed to exhaustion.

On the second evening, he called her.

"They keep asking how I feel," he said.

"And?"

"I don't know yet."

"That's a start," she said, and he exhaled—half-laugh, half-sob.

A nurse later told her he had cried that night, long and quietly.

He spoke of Baba, of unspoken grief, of the performance of strength that had finally worn through.

The nurse said it wasn't a breakdown; it was a release.

When she visited the next day, the girls brought drawings.

Anya's showed him in a superhero cape; Mira's had a giant red heart labeled "Papa's Power."

He laughed—a real laugh, uneven and alive—and Diana felt something unclench inside her chest.

He came home ten days later, thinner but lighter, as though someone had opened a window in his chest.

He cooked dinner that night—dal and rice—and they ate in near-silence, the kind that doesn't sting.

Afterward he said, "I think I need to start over."

"From what?" she asked.

He looked at her, almost grateful. "From pretending."

But healing, she knew, doesn't move in straight lines.

The black dog still lingered, patient.

Some nights it sat at the foot of their bed, invisible but undeniable.

He would wake sweating, heart racing, whispering apologies to no one.

She would rest a hand on his back until the rhythm steadied again.

The work-trip to Savannah came in early spring.

He told her it was a short conference, three nights.

She packed his shirts, slid a note into the pocket: *Remember to breathe.*

He didn't tell Diana about the meeting that night; she would only learn later, in fragments, that his first "I'm Karan" happened in a church basement in Savannah.

On the second night, after a company dinner, he walked the streets alone.

The air smelled of salt and magnolia; neon blurred in puddles from the afternoon rain.

He passed a bar, heard the laughter, and for a moment felt the gravitational pull of forgetting.

Inside, the noise was warm—glass, brass, and a temporary belonging.

He ordered one drink, then another, then stopped.

The faces around him blurred.

He felt the old hunger—the one that wasn't about alcohol at all, but about silence, relief, the impossible wish to feel whole.

Outside, he saw a small church across the street. Its basement door was open.

A cardboard sign leaned against the wall: **AA – 7 PM – All Welcome.**

He crossed over before he could change his mind.

Later Karan vividly recalled and described Diana his first meeting.

"The room smelled of burnt coffee and rain-soaked coats.

Folding chairs circled a table stacked with Styrofoam cups.

A woman in her sixties smiled and said, "First time?"

He nodded.

"Then you're right on time."

When his turn came, he stood, hands trembling slightly.

"I'm Karan," he said.

The room answered in chorus, "Hi, Karan."

He paused. "And I'm... lost."

No one looked away. No one offered pity.

Only recognition—the kind that doesn't need explanation.

Afterward a man with weathered hands patted his shoulder.

"Keep coming back," he said. "It works if you work it."

Karan didn't yet know what *it* was, but for the first time in years, he believed in the possibility of working something real."

He came home changed but not cured.

Diana couldn't name it at first—maybe humility, maybe relief.

He spoke less of work, more of mornings.

He started running again, slow laps around the block before dawn.

Sometimes, over breakfast, he mentioned the people he'd met: a trucker from Kansas, a nurse from Florida, a poet from Atlanta.

"They're all me," he said once. "Different versions."

She didn't ask for details. Some journeys required privacy.

Yet she noticed: he drank water at dinner now, not wine.

He knelt with the girls when they prayed.

He laughed more, though softly, as if testing whether joy could still hold his weight.

When his first sober anniversary arrived, he almost forgot.

It was Mira who reminded him, waving a construction-paper calendar she'd made.

"One whole year, Papa!"

He smiled, embarrassed, touched.

That evening he told Diana, "I think I've stopped running."

She looked at him, steady. "Then maybe now you can start living."

He nodded, uncertain but willing.

Outside, twilight gathered, cool and forgiving.

The maple's branches swayed like slow applause.

Later, lying beside her, he whispered, "It's still there, you know. The dog."

"I know," she said.

"But it doesn't scare me now. It just waits. And I let it."

She reached for his hand.

"Maybe that's what healing really is," she said. "Not chasing the light, just learning to sit beside the dark."

He turned toward her, eyes clear in the dimness.

"Then you've been healing me all along."

Diana didn't answer. She only smiled into the silence—the quiet grace that asks for nothing and saves everything.

The black dog retreated, but Diana knew it never really left. It just slept until called.

In the quiet of those evenings, after the girls were in bed, he sometimes talked about the meetings.

"Everyone there has a story," he said. "Different details, same gravity."

"What's yours?" she asked.

He smiled sadly. "Still writing it."

Once, after one of those talks, she asked if he was angry with her—for not stopping him sooner, or for staying.

He shook his head. "You were the only thing that didn't turn blurry."

She didn't cry, but she reached for his hand, and for the first time in months, he didn't pull away.

That spring, he told her he wanted to travel—alone.

"Nepal," he said. "I need to see where stillness isn't optional."

She wanted to say no, but the look in his eyes stopped her. It wasn't an escape. It was return.

"Then go," she said.

"And you'll be here when I come back?"

She smiled. "I always am."

The morning he left was bright and windless.

The girls had drawn him cards—mountains with smiling suns and stick-figure climbers.

Diana slipped one into his backpack when he wasn't looking.

At the airport he looked nervous, like a man walking toward both mercy and confession.

"Three weeks," he said, though his tone made it sound uncertain.

"Three weeks," she echoed.

When he turned at the gate, his face was calm in a way she hadn't seen in years—emptied, not of love, but of noise.

The house felt too large without him.

Not sad, just echoing.

The girls filled it with motion: school, music, questions, sleepovers.

Diana kept pace, but evenings stretched long once they were in bed.

She made tea, unrolled her mat, and moved through poses beneath the hum of the refrigerator.

The quiet was both ache and medicine.

Letters began arriving after ten days—short emails from Kathmandu cafés:

"The air here tastes of dust and altitude."

"Everyone walks uphill as if chasing God."

"Tell the girls the prayer flags look like flying crayons."

She read them aloud at dinner, each one proof that he was still reaching outward.

Afterward she forwarded them to herself, so they'd never disappear into spam.

At night she wondered what he saw there: men spinning prayer wheels, women lighting butter lamps, the patient rhythm of temples older than memory.

She imagined him sitting cross-legged before dawn, eyes closed, breath even—the edge and the center finally touching.

In his absence, the world rearranged itself into gentler proportions.

Mornings were smoother; she woke early, brewed coffee, packed lunches while the girls argued over cereal.

She discovered she liked the solitude between drop-off and work—a small, sacred hour when the house breathed in its own rhythm.

The maple outside had begun to bud again; its branches moved against the sky like ink strokes on water.

She started keeping a small notebook on the counter.

Not a diary—just fragments:

"Grace begins when control ends."

"Stillness isn't silence—it's trust."

They weren't mantras yet, but they steadied her hands.

The first call came from Pokhara.

Static, then his voice, thin but real.

"I hiked up to Sarangkot at sunrise," he said. "The clouds were beneath us. For a minute it felt like walking on forgiveness."

She smiled. "Maybe that's what you came for."

"Maybe," he said. Then, softer: "Tell the girls I can see forever from here."

When the line went dead, she held the phone a moment longer, as if warmth might linger in metal.

That night she dreamed of him standing at the edge of a cliff, wind tangling his hair, arms outstretched—not falling, not flying, just suspended in the thin air between fear and grace.

While he wandered through mountains, she began teaching a small yoga class at the community center.

It started informally—two coworkers asking for tips, then a notice on the bulletin board.

On Saturdays she led half a dozen women through simple sequences, her voice finding a calm authority she hadn't expected.

She didn't tell Karan yet. Some beginnings are too fragile for announcement.

The girls came once, sitting cross-legged in the corner coloring quietly.

Anya whispered, "You sound different when you talk like that."

"How?"

"Like you're listening to something we can't hear."

Diana smiled. "Maybe I am."

The last message arrived the day before he flew home:

"Tomorrow Kathmandu → Amsterdam → MSP. I'm bringing prayer beads, not answers. Maybe that's better. I love you."

She printed it and placed it on the fridge beside his earlier note about what they'd built.

Two versions of him—one leaving, one returning.

At the airport, when he finally appeared beyond customs, she almost didn't recognize him.

His beard had grown, his frame leaner.

But his eyes—clear, steady—were the same.

The girls barreled into his arms, laughter cutting through the din.

He lifted them both, staggered under their weight, then looked at Diana over their shoulders.

"Still here," she said.

"Always," he answered.

On the drive home he told stories: monks and laughter, rivers the color of stone, a boy who offered him tea and refused payment.

But under the words lay something quieter—a peace that didn't need proof.

When they reached the house, he paused on the porch, breathing the cold Midwestern air as if tasting it anew.

"Everything smells different," he said.

"It's spring," she replied.

"No," he said gently. "It's me."

That night, after the girls slept, they sat together in the dim kitchen.

Between them, his prayer beads coiled on the table like a small river.

"I didn't find answers," he said.

"I didn't expect you to."

"I did learn one thing."

She waited.

"That silence doesn't always mean despair. Sometimes it's just... clearing space."

She nodded. "Then keep it clear."

He reached across the table, his hand resting over hers.

The gesture was light, uncertain, yet enough.

Outside, the wind moved through the maple, new leaves whispering against the glass.

For the first time in months, she didn't feel the house holding its breath.

Later, as they climbed into bed, he said quietly, "When I was up there, I kept thinking about balance."

"Yoga?" she teased.

"Life," he said. "It's not about standing still. It's about adjusting every second without falling."

She smiled in the dark. "Then we're both learning."

In the weeks that followed, life didn't transform so much as deepen.

Karan attended meetings twice a week, spoke less but listened more.

He volunteered at the shelter downtown, helped fix leaky faucets, and carried crates of food.

Diana's yoga class grew; she began taking certification modules online after the girls were asleep.

Sometimes, they met in the middle of the night—him returning from a meeting, her closing her laptop—and sat on the porch in silence.

No grand declarations. Just breath, shared under a sky that finally seemed wide enough for both of them.

One evening in late summer, he brought her a gift: a small clay bowl from Bhaktapur, the glaze the color of rain.

"For your altar," he said.

"I don't have one."

"You will."

She placed it by the window where the first light would find it each morning.

When he turned to go, she touched his arm.

"Does the black dog still follow?"

He paused. "Sometimes. But now I walk it before it walks me."

Diana smiled, and for the first time, the answer felt whole.

Chapter 12
The Edge and the Center
Healing is not arrival, but returning without fear.

By spring, the house had settled into a gentler rhythm.

The air itself seemed lighter, as if someone had opened all the windows and let the years of silence drift out.

Karan rose early again—sometimes before dawn—making coffee, reading in the stillness.

The dark circles under his eyes had faded; laughter returned slowly, like a muscle learning to move.

He went to meetings twice a week and never spoke about them unless she asked.

When he did, his voice carried the calm of someone who no longer needed to prove survival.

Diana, too, had changed.

Her yoga class at the community center had grown from six to fifteen; the city offered her a small stipend to teach twice a week.

At work, her team's pilot project in product innovation succeeded beyond expectations.

Her supervisor said she had a "steady grace under pressure," a phrase that made her think of all the mornings she'd stood at the edge of her own unraveling and chosen composure anyway.

Anya joined the school orchestra, Mira discovered soccer, and weekends filled with bleachers and folding chairs. Both in the swim team and figure skating club. Life hummed of fullness.

Karan volunteered as a timekeeper, clipboard in hand, pretending to know the rules.

He was good with the other parents—still quiet, but approachable, the kind of calm that made people linger in conversation.

Sometimes Diana caught him watching their daughters with a look she recognized: gratitude mixed with disbelief.

Like someone who had come close to losing the light and now couldn't stop studying it.

They started attending church again.

Not out of obligation, but rhythm.

The pastor spoke of service and patience; the choir sang hymns that trembled on the edge of joy.

Diana liked how Karan listened—not as a believer, but as someone open to awe.

Afterward they'd drive to a diner for pancakes, the girls arguing over syrup.

These were the small sacraments she learned to count as grace.

That summer, Diana suggested India.

"Not for anyone else," she said. "For the four of us."

Karan looked at her, surprised. "Are you sure?"

She nodded. "It's time."

They flew out of Minneapolis on a bright December afternoon—Minneapolis to Paris, Paris to New Delhi.

Anya claimed the window seat, Mira fell asleep before take-off, and Karan watched the flight map with a quiet intensity, as if each glowing line might tether him homeward.

From Delhi they connected to Bhopal—his first return to the house he had grown up in since Baba's death.

Aai and Tai met them at the airport, surrounded by a small procession of neighbors.

Garlands, laughter, tears.

The air smelled of dust, rain, and coriander.

The old house stood proud and worn—veranda sagging, bougainvillea spilling over the wall and Ashoka trees along the fence, pretending to guard what was inside.

When Diana stepped through the gate, a gust of wind carried the scent of jasmine and kerosene, and she felt time bend.

Inside, photographs lined the corridor: faces she half-recognized from Karan's stories.

Aai's eyes shone as she introduced her grandchildren to every detail—the swing Baba had built, the mango tree that still bore fruit.

Neighbors drifted in all afternoon—plates of poha and laddoos, laughter layered with memory.

Karan moved among them, touching feet, accepting blessings, translating fragments for Diana and the girls until he gave up.

"Too many," he said, smiling. "Just remember, everyone here once spanked me."

The girls squealed; Aai pretended not to understand English and laughed anyway.

That evening, the rooftop filled with voices.

Someone played an old flute; the air hummed with electricity.

Diana sat beside Aai, sipping chai, watching lightning ripple across the lake.

It felt like sitting inside a heartbeat.

A week later they took the early train back to Delhi, and from there boarded the *Palace on Wheels*—seven days, seven cities, a dream unfolding on iron tracks.

The carriage gleamed with brass lamps and embroidered curtains.

Anya and Mira bounced from bunk to bunk, whispering conspiracies of snacks and window seats.

Karan watched them, eyes full of quiet astonishment.

Diana took his hand. "You look twelve," she said.

"Feels like it," he answered.

They met two other families early on—one from Melbourne, another from Pittsburgh—Indian emigrants like themselves, orbiting familiar accents in unfamiliar worlds.

Diana found comfort in the symmetry: shared childhood foods, shared exile.

They spoke of airports, grandparents, identity—the visible and invisible struggles of belonging.

Listening, she realized that immigration wasn't a single crossing but a lifelong balancing act between memory and invention.

Each day brought color and motion:

Jaipur's pink stone glowing under morning sun, elephants swaying toward Amber Fort;

Jodhpur, where the walls caught the light like flame;

Udaipur's mirrored lakes;

Agra, where even the girls went silent before the Taj.

But Jaisalmer was her favorite—

a fort rising golden from the desert, still and eternal, fifty kilometers from the border.

They rode camels through dunes that shimmered like waves, the wind carrying sand that felt ancient as salt.

That night, under a vault of stars, local musicians sang in a language she didn't know but somehow understood.

Karan's laughter joined the rhythm, pure and unguarded.

For the first time in years, she saw the boy he must have been—the dreamer before the grief, the edge before the fall.

Back in Delhi, they spent a final day wandering Connaught Place, buying trinkets and tea for the flight home.

Anya bargained for bangles, Mira for a drum; Karan bought prayer beads for Diana, though she already had her own.

They flew Delhi to Amsterdam, Amsterdam to Minneapolis—time zones folding like origami.

When the plane touched down, the girls pressed their faces to the window.

"Home," Anya whispered.

"Both," Diana said. "Always both."

Karan had transitioned into a healthcare nonprofit the few years before, consulting on access and food-equity programs. Karan's healthcare nonprofit went remote; the girls' school moved online; Diana's yoga classes turned into pixelated squares on a laptop.

The rhythms they had rebuilt twisted into something smaller and strangely tender.

Karan set up his desk by the window overlooking the maple.

Anya practiced violin in her room, Mira chased the cat through hallways, Diana led virtual sessions from the living room, her calm voice carrying through the house like a prayer.

Outside, sirens wailed some days, silence others.

Inside, they learned the texture of stillness: shared breakfasts, long walks, evenings of board games and laughter that felt almost guilty.

The world spun in chaos, yet within their walls, something held.

Late one night, after the girls had gone to bed, Karan stood at the window watching snow begin to fall.

"This could all end tomorrow," he said softly.

Diana joined him, shoulder to shoulder. "Then we've already lived enough today."

He turned, kissed her forehead, and whispered, "The edge feels different now."

She smiled. "That's because you finally found the center."

Outside, the frost glittered under the streetlight—silent, everywhere at once.

Inside, the house breathed—steady, luminous, alive.

Chapter 13
The Body Remembers
The body keeps the prayers the mind forgets.

The house had grown used to quiet.

By early spring, even silence had a rhythm: coffee brewing, violin scales from upstairs, the soft thud of a yoga mat unrolling.

Diana was reading in the living room one evening, curled beneath a blanket, a novel resting lightly on her knees.

Outside, the last of the snow was melting; water dripped from the eaves in slow, steady intervals.

She felt a flicker of motion above her head—a shadow moving just beyond the edge of sight.

She glanced up, saw nothing, returned to her book.

Then came the *whoosh*—a sudden sweep of air close to her face, followed by another.

Diana froze.

A dark shape circled the ceiling, its path frantic and erratic.

It took her a moment to understand: a bat.

Inside.

Her breath caught.

She pulled the blanket over her head and began to shout for Karan.

Upstairs, she heard a door open, footsteps, his calm voice calling, "What happened?"

"Bat!" she yelled from under the blanket. "Bat! There's a bat in the house!"

Anya and Mira screamed from their rooms.

Doors slammed.

The house erupted in small, chaotic shrieks.

Karan descended the stairs laughing.

"Relax," he said, scanning the room. "It's only a bat."

"Only?" Diana peered out, incredulous.

"It's flying in circles like it owns the place!"

He grinned. "My uncle in Belgaum used to keep pet bats. They're harmless. The trick is to let them sit. Their hind legs are too short—once they land, they can't take off easily."

As if summoned by memory, the creature fluttered once more, then dropped behind the long curtain near the patio door.

Karan nodded toward it. "There you go. He's done."

He disappeared into the laundry room, returned with a towel, and approached the curtain gently, speaking as though to a guest.

Diana watched, heart still thudding, while he lifted the fabric slowly.

The bat clung there, small and trembling, its wings folded tight.

With the towel he cupped it—steady, deliberate—and walked toward the back door.

The night air was cool and clear.

He opened his hands, and the bat vanished into the dark, a quick blur against the moonlight.

When he came back inside, he tossed the towel in the wash and clapped his hands once.

"There," he said. "Done."

Anya and Mira crept down the stairs.

"Is it gone?" Anya whispered.

"Free," Karan said.

Mira giggled. "Dad's Batman!"

Laughter rippled through the house, soft but contagious.

Diana stood, still wrapped in her blanket, half exasperated, half in awe.

She crossed the room and kissed him on the cheek.

"Twenty-two years," she said, "and you finally live up to your favorite superhero."

He smiled, that rare, mischievous spark in his eyes.

"Better late than never."

Later that night, after the girls had gone to bed, Diana sat beside him on the couch, the house calm again.

The window was cracked open, the air faint with thaw and pine.

She looked at him—the same man who once couldn't climb out of his own darkness—and thought how steady he'd become.

Not fixed, not changed, but centered.

Where once there had been tension, now there was patience; where silence once meant withdrawal, it now meant peace.

Karan leaned back, eyes half closed.

"You know," he said, "I think we were all that bat tonight. Just trying to find a way out."

She laughed. "And you, as usual, were the one who opened the window."

He shook his head. "No. You were. I just followed the light."

Diana looked around—the familiar furniture, the quiet hum of the heater, the faint glow from the kitchen nightlight.

She felt it then, not as a revelation but as recognition: grace wasn't distant anymore.

It was here, folded into the fabric of ordinary evenings, breathing through laughter and laundry and small rescues.

Her own body had begun to change with that knowing.

She felt it in the ease of her shoulders, the length of her breath, the clarity that arrived when she moved through her yoga sequences in the early light.

Each pose was no longer a performance but a prayer.

Her teaching had grown—virtual classes, workshops, a small but devoted community that saw her not just as an instructor but as a presence.

She found herself guiding others through the same balance she'd been learning all along: how to stand without stiffening, how to fall without fear.

Some mornings, Karan would pass behind her, coffee in hand, and pause at the doorway, watching.

"Your students have no idea you're preaching," he'd say.

She smiled. "That's the point."

Their daughters flourished—Anya entering high school, Mira painting murals on her bedroom wall.

The world outside remained uncertain, but within these walls, there was enough light to navigate by.

Sometimes, as they sat on the porch at dusk, Diana would glance at Karan, and he'd meet her eyes with that same quiet understanding:

that life, at its truest, was never about escaping the dark—but learning, again and again, to hold it gently and let it fly.

As the months passed, Diana found herself drawn more deeply into her practice.

What had begun as routine—thirty minutes before work, an hour on weekends—slowly became ritual.

Her mat was no longer just fabric and foam; it was a threshold.

Each morning she stepped onto it, she felt the distance between breath and thought narrow until there was only stillness.

She enrolled in a 200-hour yoga teacher training course online—early mornings before the girls woke, late nights after Karan's meetings.

She studied anatomy, philosophy, and the lineage of breath.

At first, she felt like an imposter.

Then, slowly, something shifted.

Her body began to remember what her mind had forgotten: that wisdom is not earned by knowing but by listening.

During one session, the instructor said, "Grace isn't the absence of struggle. It's the presence of awareness within it."

Diana wrote the sentence down and underlined it three times.

It felt like an answer she hadn't realized she'd been asking for.

By summer, she received her certification—a modest PDF in her inbox, but to her, it was a consecration.

She began offering classes outdoors, beneath the maple tree in their yard.

A circle of mats on the grass.

Women from the neighborhood came—mothers, teachers, retirees.

Sometimes Mira joined, copying poses with comic seriousness; sometimes Anya brought her violin and played softly at the end of class.

The air filled with the scent of cut grass and something larger—trust, maybe, or release.

Karan watched from the porch those mornings, coffee in hand, smiling.

"You've built your own temple," he said once.

"Not mine," she answered. "Ours."

In the evenings, she wrote reflections in the same notebook she'd started when he was away in Nepal.

The pages had grown dense with fragments—half prayers, half observations:

"Stillness is not what's left when motion ends; it's what's beneath it."

"Some days I am the wave, some days I am the shore."

"The body remembers what the mind denies."

The last line became her quiet mantra.

When she guided her students through slow movement, she spoke it softly:

"Let your body remember what safety feels like."

And in those words, she was speaking to herself.

Her work at the food company evolved too.

Years of precision in the lab had given way to management, mentoring, and connection.

She found herself listening more, advising young analysts the way her old mentors once had.

One of them—a bright, uncertain woman—confessed after a meeting, "You're the calmest person I've ever seen."

Diana smiled. "Calm is just another word for practiced."

That evening, she told Karan about it.

He laughed. "They should see you when there's a bat in the room."

She threw a napkin at him, and they both dissolved into laughter—the easy, breathless kind that carries no residue.

He reached across the table, brushed her hand.

"Do you ever think about how far we've come?"

She nodded. "Sometimes I think we never moved at all. We just learned how to stand still better."

He grinned. "That's very... yogic of you."

She leaned closer. "That's very grateful of you."

And in the quiet that followed, they didn't need to speak of recovery, or loss, or what might come next.

They had finally learned the language of enough.

Autumn arrived with its old precision: maple leaves gold and crisp, school routines resuming, the world tilting back toward normal.

And one night, over dinner, Karan looked up from his plate and said,

"What would you think about going back to India—all of us this time?"

Diana paused, fork halfway to her mouth.

"Now?"

"Now," he said simply. "Before life gets loud again."

She smiled.

"Then let's go."

Outside, wind moved through the trees, scattering leaves across the porch.

Inside, the girls were laughing in the kitchen, arguing over whose turn it was to feed the cat.

Karan watched them, then looked at her.

"What are you thinking?" he asked.

"That the center isn't still," she said. "It's alive."

He nodded, eyes bright.

"Then maybe it's time to find it again—together."

And just like that, grace changed direction.

Chapter 14
The Still Storm
When the world stops, the heart learns its shape.

The world stopped.

Not with thunder, but with silence.

It began as a whisper on the news—distant, improbable.

Then, suddenly, it was everywhere.

Flights grounded. Schools shuttered. Offices emptied.

The familiar rhythm of departure and return vanished.

The house became the whole map.

Kitchen, office, classroom, sanctuary.

They drew invisible borders between spaces—this corner for work, that one for prayer, the couch for meetings, the porch for breathing.

At first, chaos ruled.

Anya's violin competed with Mira's virtual science lab.

Karan's voice drifted from upstairs: muted, unmuted, apologizing for echo.

Diana's yoga students froze mid-pose when the Wi-Fi faltered.

Everyone adjusted. Then readjusted. Then surrendered.

Weeks turned into months.

The stillness became a kind of teacher.

They learned the dimensions of their home by sound:

The squeak of the hallway floorboard, the hum of the fridge, the way silence carried through open doors.

Even the cat moved differently—less restless, more reverent.

Outside, sirens cut through the evenings like hymns.

Inside, they listened—sometimes praying, sometimes only breathing.

Each day ended with a meal, imperfect but shared.

They no longer rushed.

Conversation wandered.

Laughter returned, tentative at first, then bold.

Anya practiced Bach until the strings frayed.

Mira painted constellations on her ceiling, naming each one after the family: "Mama's Nebula," "Karan's Comet."

Karan planted basil and mint on the windowsill, narrating their growth as if they were students.

Diana taught yoga through a laptop perched on cookbooks.

Her voice reached living rooms she would never see.

"Breathe," she said each morning. "Not because the world is safe, but because you are here."

Some nights, when the girls were asleep, Karan and Diana sat on the floor against the couch, candles flickering between them.

The world outside was quiet except for wind in the maple and the distant hum of a generator.

Karan said once, "It feels like the whole planet is holding its breath."

Diana answered, "Then we breathe for it."

There were hard days, too.

Headlines heavy with loss.

Phone calls that ended in static and grief.

Friends who vanished behind hospital walls.

Diana lit a candle for each name she knew, whispering no words—just presence.

On those days, Karan moved slower.

Sometimes he stood at the window for hours, watching the empty street, tracing patterns in condensation.

Other times, he cooked—complex curries, slow stews, recipes that filled the air for hours.

Cooking, she realized, had become his way of praying.

They spoke often about small things.

The way light fell through blinds.

The smell of rain on concrete.

The memory of open airports.

It wasn't escape; it was gratitude rehearsed aloud.

By midsummer, the world had grown quieter still.

Birdsong seemed louder.

Evenings stretched long and gold.

Neighbors waved from porches instead of passing by.

The air, scrubbed of haste, felt honest.

Anya built a makeshift fort in the living room and declared it a "peace zone."

Mira drew on the windows with washable markers: *Everything grows again.*

They left the words up for weeks.

Each time Diana passed them, she smiled.

She found her body softening too—hips looser, breath slower, heart less defensive.

Grace, she thought, wasn't an achievement.

It was endurance without bitterness.

Some mornings she taught yoga at sunrise on the back porch.

Karan would join, sitting cross-legged with his coffee, pretending not to follow along.

Afterward, they'd walk barefoot through dew-damp grass, careful not to speak too soon, as if words might disturb the fragile peace between them.

Once, he said quietly, "I used to think peace meant stillness."

"And now?"

"Now I think it means presence."

She smiled. "Then we're finally learning the same language."

Autumn returned, but without its usual urgency.

The girls started remote school again, now veterans of routine.

The maple outside the window blazed scarlet, then shed its leaves all at once—as if cleansing itself of the year.

One night, as the first snow began to fall, Diana stood at the window, holding a mug of tea gone cold.

Karan came beside her, wrapping an arm around her waist.

They watched the flakes drift down, soft and soundless.

"It's strange," she said. "The world fell apart, and somehow we found ourselves."

He nodded. "Maybe it had to stop for us to hear again."

The clock ticked, slow and steady.

Somewhere upstairs, Mira laughed in her sleep.

Diana closed her eyes and listened.

The storm, she realized, had never been outside.

It had been within them all along—years of rushing, proving, reaching.

Now, at last, it was still.

Chapter 15
Lighthouse
Steadiness is a kind of radiance.

The world opened again—cautiously, unevenly, as if remembering how to breathe.

Airports hummed. Schools filled. Traffic returned.

But for Diana, noise no longer equaled life.

She moved through the renewed clamor as one might move through a dream—grateful, but unwilling to rush.

At the food company, she returned to in-person meetings and fluorescent light.

Old hierarchies reassembled, the chatter resumed.

Yet something in her had shifted.

She no longer mistook busyness for purpose.

Her calmness unnerved people at first. Then they began to seek it.

A junior analyst once asked, "How do you stay so steady?"

Diana smiled. "Practice. And perspective."

Outside those walls, she was building her own.

Her yoga community had grown during lockdown—students who stayed even after screens turned to space again.

On Saturday mornings, she taught in the park by the river.

Children played nearby, leaves rustled overhead, and the smell of grass mixed with incense.

"Breathe," she'd say, "as though the world is already forgiving you."

Karan's restlessness returned, but this time it had direction.

The pandemic had stripped away his old illusions of permanence.

He'd tasted quiet; now he wanted meaning.

One evening he told her, "I think it's time to start something new."

"New like what?" she asked.

"Something that matters," he said. "Something that doesn't vanish with funding."

She nodded. She had heard that tone before—the one that once led him to exhaustion.

But this time, it sounded different.

Less driven, more alive.

He left the company within three months.

Started consulting for a nonprofit that connected hospitals with rural clinics.

Then a second project—data tools for vulnerable populations.

Then a third—his own small firm.

The work spread quickly, word by word, person by person.

He built quietly, methodically, the way a man rebuilds trust in himself.

Diana watched him from the doorway some nights—shoulders relaxed, voice even, eyes clear.

He no longer chased brilliance.

He simply followed usefulness.

The rhythm of their home changed again, but gently this time.

Mornings began with shared coffee and silence.

Afternoons brought motion—calls, projects, yoga classes, violin lessons, laughter, deadlines.

Evenings found them on the porch, sometimes talking, sometimes not.

The space between words had become its own kind of intimacy.

Once, while watching the sunset, he said, "You know what I realized? You've always been the lighthouse."

She laughed. "Meaning?"

"When I drift too far, you don't pull me back—you just keep shining until I find the shore."

She smiled. "And what if you stop looking?"

He thought for a long moment. "Then I hope you shine anyway."

"I always do."

Anya entered her final year of high school; Mira discovered photography.

Their house filled with college brochures, camera lenses, piano music, and late-night snacks.

Diana marveled at how the same walls that once held toddlers' laughter now echoed with teenage debate.

Every phase, she thought, had its own kind of grace.

Sometimes she caught Karan watching the girls, pride softening his face.

Once, he whispered, "They saved me."

"No," she said gently. "You did the saving. They just gave you a reason."

By spring, the garden bloomed again—basil, mint, lavender, tomatoes climbing wire frames.

Karan joked that the plants were his real coworkers.

Diana teased that they listened better.

But when she watered them, she whispered thanks under her breath.

They had seen everything—the storms, the stillness, the rebuilding.

One evening, as twilight deepened, she found him outside, tinkering with a solar light fixture near the path.

"Trying to fix it again?" she asked.

He looked up, smiling. "Just making sure it stays on through the night."

She stepped beside him, hand brushing his.

"Then we match," she said.

He laughed softly. "Always the lighthouse."

"And you," she said, "the one who finally learned to look up."

The yard fell quiet except for the soft hum of crickets.

Above them, the first stars appeared—steady, unhurried, unafraid of dark.

For the first time in years, Diana felt no need to interpret life, only to inhabit it.

Grace, she thought, had never been a destination.

It was light—constant, quiet, guiding everything home.

Chapter 16
The Solstice

Every turning holds its own kind of grace.

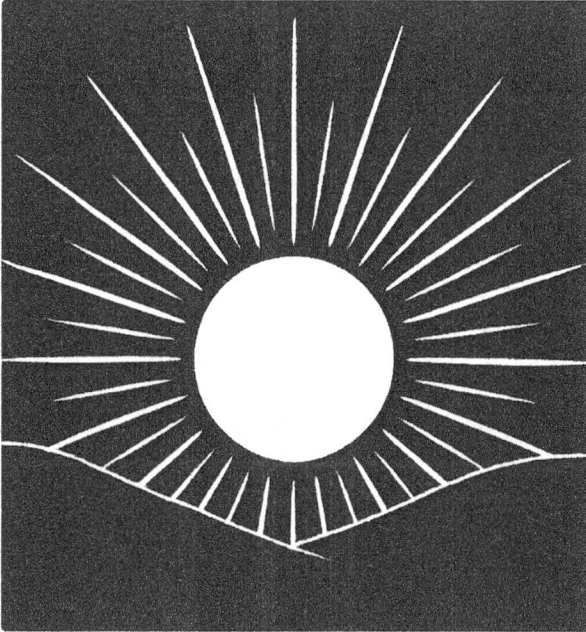

Summer lingered longer that year, as if reluctant to move on.

Light stayed late, pouring gold through the kitchen window until the maple cast its shadow across the floor.

The house smelled of basil, sunscreen, and change.

Anya's acceptance letter came on a Tuesday.

University of Minnesota — scholarship, dorm assignment, the map of a new beginning.

She read it aloud once, then again, voice trembling between pride and disbelief.

Mira filmed it on her phone, shouting, "She's leaving us!" and laughing through tears.

Karan opened his arms and both girls collided into him, a tangle of limbs and future.

Diana stood a step behind, smiling, memorizing the moment.

The world had paused once before; now it was spinning again.

That summer became a catalogue of small lasts.

Last family movie night.

Last violin lesson at the community center.

Last time four toothbrushes lined the bathroom sink.

Diana folded each memory like laundry, smoothing it carefully before setting it aside.

The morning they drove to the dorms, the air was clear, edges crisp.

Boxes filled the trunk, snacks in the backseat.

Mira sang from the radio until they reached the river.

Then silence — not tense, just full.

At the campus curb, students swarmed, parents carried, everyone pretending not to cry.

Karan handled the heavy boxes; Diana made the bed twice.

Anya hugged them quickly, bravely.

When she turned to wave, sunlight caught her hair — the same gold that once framed her first steps.

Driving home, no one spoke.

Halfway there, Karan reached across the console, took Diana's hand.

"She's ready," he said.

"I know."

"You are too."

She smiled faintly. "That's the harder part."

Back home, Mira had already claimed the upstairs room.

"Studio," she declared, holding her camera like a passport.

She filled it with light strings, thrifted furniture, and taped prints to every wall.

The house, though quieter, didn't feel emptier — only rearranged.

Karan's work was thriving; Diana's classes were steady.

They talked about visiting India again, about maybe moving closer to the cities when the girls were grown.

But most evenings they stayed on the porch, content to watch the day dissolve.

Once, as the sky deepened into indigo, Diana said,

"It feels like standing between seasons."

Karan nodded. "That's what a solstice is — not summer or winter, just the turning."

She liked that. The turning. The pause before the next motion.

Autumn returned in shades of copper.

Anya called weekly — stories of roommates, cafeteria food, midnight debates.

Mira's photographs began winning small contests; she framed them with thrift-store wood and hung them in the hallway.

Karan and Diana walked together in the evenings, their shadows long and parallel.

Sometimes she felt a quiet ache, not sadness, but space — a widening of the life she once filled with tending.

It surprised her how calm it was.

Love, she thought, doesn't vanish when it leaves the house.

It just learns new addresses.

One night, the first frost arrived.

Diana stepped outside barefoot, her breath visible.

The sky shimmered clear as glass.

Through the window she saw Karan reading, Mira editing photos, the kettle steaming.

The scene glowed warm behind the cold pane, like a lantern in snow.

She whispered a small prayer—not for protection, but for presence.

For continued light, whatever the distance.

Later, lying beside Karan, she listened to the faint tick of the clock.

He murmured, half asleep, "You're quiet."

"Just listening."

"To what?"

"The turning."

He smiled without opening his eyes. "It's gentle this time."

"It should be," she said. "We worked for that."

And in the dark, with winter waiting beyond the glass, Diana felt a peace that needed no story—

only breath,

and time,

and the steady grace of staying luminous while everything else moves.

Epilogue

Grace

Presence is the light that survives the night.

Dawn arrived like forgiveness—slow, certain, and without needing to announce itself.

The sky, still half-dreaming, opened in shades of rose and gray.

Mist lifted from the river, the air cool and patient.

Diana spread her mat on the wooden platform outside the community hall, dew gathering along the edges.

A few students were already there, quiet silhouettes arranging themselves in the soft light.

The world was waking, but gently.

She closed her eyes, hands at her heart, and exhaled.

"Let's begin," she said. The words left her lips like steam rising in the cool morning.

The sequence unfolded like memory—breath to motion, motion to stillness.

The body remembering what peace felt like before it had a name.

Each inhale carried the weight of years; each exhale released it.

She looked up once—the maple beyond the fence trembled with light, its new leaves translucent.

The sound of the town stirring in the distance felt like the ocean's slow return.

When the class ended, she sat cross-legged facing the sunrise.

The others lingered, rolling mats softly, reluctant to disturb the quiet.

Someone whispered, "It's so calm here."

Diana smiled. "That's because we stopped trying to earn it."

She remained after they left, alone with the river's shimmer and the faint scent of incense drifting from her bag.

A sparrow landed on the railing, cocked its head, and flew away again.

The moment was so brief it felt eternal.

She thought of Karan—still asleep, probably, curled toward the warmth.

Of Anya in her dorm, Mira in her half-finished darkroom.

Of all the versions of herself she had outgrown but never abandoned.

Life, she knew now, was not a straight line but a tide.

It pulled away.

It returned.

And what stayed behind—the sand, the shells, the quiet shimmer—was its own kind of grace.

She rose, folded her mat, and lingered a moment longer.

The sun crested the hill, gold light spilling through the trees.

She lifted her face toward it, eyes closed, and whispered the words she told her students every morning:

"Breathe in what remains.

Breathe out what no longer serves.

Stay where you are.

That is enough."

The wind moved through her hair like a benediction.

The world, reborn in light, exhaled with her.

And for one clear instant—no striving, no memory, no edge or center—

Only presence.
Only grace.

About the Author

Chetan (Chet) Rao is a scientist, investor, entrepreneur, mentor, inventor, and founder — a bridge between worlds of logic and light. His work moves through science, technology, and human understanding, grounded in the belief that invention gains its worth only when it serves compassion.

Educated at the University of Wisconsin, the University of Minnesota, and the Indian Institute of Technology Bombay, Chet has led and advised global organizations across healthcare and consumer innovation. His research and leadership reflect a lifelong pursuit of meaning — where systems meet stories, and where insight becomes empathy.

Through The Weight Trilogy, Chet explores that same boundary — between self and soul, certainty and surrender — tracing the unseen forces that connect creation, consciousness, and grace.

"Between knowing and understanding lies the weight of being."

— Chetan Rao

Books In This Series

The Weight Trilogy traces a single life through three distinct ways of seeing: from the edge, from the center, and from above.

Spanning generations, loss, love, and spiritual insight, the trilogy reveals how perspective transforms everything we carry.

Book I — **The Weight of Shadows**: A story of searching and survival, where meaning is glimpsed at the margins.

Book II — **The Weight of Grace**: A story of connection and presence, seen through the quiet illumination of love.

Book III — **The Weight of Nothing**: A story of release and transcendence, where silence becomes its own kind of truth.

Together, these books form a meditation on what it means to be human — to break, to heal, and to return to ourselves.